USING THE DOG TYPE SYSTEM IN YOUR EVERYDAY LIFE

Even More Ways to Gain Insights and Advice from Your Dogs

by Gini Graham Scott, Ph.D.
Author of *Do You Look Like Your Dog?*

USING THE DOG TYPE SYSTEM IN YOUR EVERYDAY LIFE

Copyright © 2017 by Gini Graham Scott

All rights reserved. No part of this book may be used or reproduced by any means, graphic, electronic, or mechanical, including photocopying, recording, taping or by any information storage retrieval system without the written permission of the author except in the case of brief quotations embodied in critical articles and reviews.

TABLE OF CONTENTS

INTRODUCTION 5
CHAPTER 1: USING THE DOG TYPE SYSTEM IN
EVERYDAY LIFE 7
   Get Some Extra Help from a Rescue Dog........................... 7
   Overcome Stress and Tension... 9
   Increase Your Energy and Feel Less Tired 11
   Increase Your Feelings of Confidence and Self-Esteem... 14
   Set and Achieve Goals 19
   An Example of How to Use the System........................... 26
CHAPTER 2: OTHER WAYS OF USING THE DOG TYPE
SYSTEM... 31
   Increase Your Skills 31
   Increase Your Creativity 34
   Solve Problems and Make Decisions 42
   Use Your Intuition to Make Better Decisions.................. 45
   New Ways to Just Have Fun 53
   Still Other Ways to Work with the Dog Type System..... 54
CHAPTER 3: SUMMING UP AND EVEN MORE
POSSIBILITIES 57
   For Self-Understanding and Personal Development........ 57
   For Understanding and Improving Relationships 59
   For a Variety of Everyday Purposes 60
   Mostly Just for Fun 60
   Still Other Ways to Use this System for Getting to Know Others
and Having Fun 61
ABOUT THE AUTHOR 63

INTRODUCTION

USING THE DOG TYPE SYSTEM IN YOUR EVERYDAY LIFE is the fourth in a series of books on using the Dog Type system for more success in your personal and work life.

Previous books introduced the Dog Profiles to better understand yourself and others. The books provided techniques for gaining help from your Top Dog, Watch Dog, Underdog, Guard Dog, and Power Dogs. You can also call on your Rescue Dog for additional help, such as for confidence and self-esteem.

This book features ways to get extra help to overcome stress and tension, increase your energy, become more confident, and set and achieve goals. Other topics covered include:
- increasing your skills,
- becoming more creative,
- solving problems and making decisions,
- new ways to have fun.

Finally, you'll see tips on gaining more self-understanding and improving relationships,

CHAPTER 1: USING THE DOG TYPE SYSTEM IN EVERYDAY LIFE

Once you know the basics of using the Dog Type system to understand yourself and others, you can apply it in multiple ways in your everyday life. Essentially, you call on your Guide Dogs and Top Dog for advice and guidance in daily life and on your Power Dogs for additional power and support in different situations. The process of visualization, mental imagery, self-talk, and other techniques allow you to tap into your intuitive, creative powers; and the relationship you develop with different types of dogs helps to increase that power. In short, wherever you call on your inner powers for advice, strength, and support – from making decisions and solving problems to practicing skills and becoming more creative – you can call on your dogs for help.

Get Some Extra Help from a Rescue Dog

A Rescue Dog is one you call that has additional qualities you feel will be helpful in a particular situation. Later, you can continue to call on that Rescue Dog for help when that situation arises again.

For example, say you feel you need to relax more, and the dogs you have already selected as your Guide Dogs, Top Dog, or Power Dogs, are hard driving, aggressive, strong dogs, usually fast and on the go – not the kind of dogs you associate with relaxing and chilling out. So now it's time to bring in a different type of dog with the needed qualities as your "Rescue Dog" to come to your "rescue".

In some cases, this helpful Rescue Dog may even be your Underdog, because you don't normally have these qualities, but could develop them. But that's fine. You can get help from all sorts of unexpected places.

You find a Rescue Dog using the same techniques for connecting with your Guide Dogs, Top Dog, and Power Dog. The difference is that you are calling on your Rescue Dog for additional help in a particular situation.

First think of what help you need or of what goal you want to accomplish. Then think of what type of dog you associate with that kind of activity. An image or the name of this dog may come to mind immediately, if you are familiar with this system. Or take a few minutes to relax, think of the situation in which you need help, and ask for your Rescue Dog to appear to help you, and soon your dog will.

For instance, say you want to increase your energy. You might visualize a Greyhound or Whippet, which are very fast dogs; then call on that dog to appear in your mind's eye or sit beside you to give you an infusion of energy. Or suppose you want to relax and calm down. You might call on an English Sheepdog or Puli, which is a very calm, relaxed dog. The Puli even looks like a huge pillow of fur you can sink into to get really relaxed. Or say you are going to a meeting where you have to be very assertive to stand up for what you want to persuade others to go along with you. The image of a Mastiff or Pit Bull might help.

In some cases, you may already have a Power Dog, Top Dog, or Watch Dog, that is ideal for helping in a particular situation. Then, simply call on your Power Dog, Top Dog, or Watch Dog to help. But if you don't already have the type of dog best suited to help in that situation, that's when you need to call on a Rescue Dog – or a team of them – to appear on the scene with the qualities and assistance you need.

Following are a variety of ways to apply these methods with your Guide Dogs, Top Dog, Power Dogs, or Rescue Dogs. As you continue working with these techniques and get to know the different dogs even better, you'll find still other ways to use these dogs and these techniques – the subject of future books in this series.

This chapter focuses on techniques for overcoming stress and tension, increasing your energy, feeling more confidence and self-esteem, and achieving your goals. The next deals with ways to increase your skills and creativity, solve problems, and make better decisions.

Overcome Stress and Tension

With many people complaining about too much stress, given today's fast paced, competitive life, calling on your dogs can help you relax and get rid of unwanted tension. You need the appropriate balance so you aren't over-tense or overstressed, and are sufficiently relaxed to feel confident, composed, and carry out any task smoothly and efficiently.

Here are some ways to do this.

Create a Mental Trigger with Your Dog for Yourself

You can use a mental trigger to help you relax. First, use a visualization or self-talk to think of a dog that suggests relaxation to you. Then whenever you feel tense or feel sensations of stress coming on, you can use the trigger to remain calm and relaxed or quickly calm down.

To create this trigger, take a few minutes to get very relaxed, and as you do, think of a dog you associate with being relaxed (such as a Beagle, English Shepherd, or Puli).Then, repeat this process a few times a day over the next few days, and each time you relax, think of this kind of dog. Eventually, just thinking of this type of dog will relax you, since you have created a conditioned response by making an association between relaxation and this dog. Once you have created this association, think of this dog any time you want to relax, and you can use this same process to create an association between any other activity and a selected dog.

Use a Relaxing Visualization with Your Dog to Help You Calm Down.

Another approach to calming down is to take a few minutes in a quiet place to visualize yourself in a relaxed setting with your Top Dog, Guide Dogs, or Rescue Dog you associate with getting relaxed.

Then, see yourself engaging in an enjoyable and relaxing activity with this dog, such as going to the beach and walking by the water or taking a leisurely walk in a sunny meadow. As you participate in this activity, feel yourself getting more and more relaxed, and if you want, have your Top Dog, Guide Dog, or Rescue Dog repeat the words to you: "Relax...Relax...You are getting more and more relaxed, more and more relaxed."

Keep doing this exercise for a few minutes, and you'll experience your body feeling more and more relaxed, too. So after a few minutes, you should feel much calmer, as well as more refreshed and reenergized.

Chase Away Your Anxieties with Your Dog to Help You Calm Down

You can chase away the anxiety you feel about something you have to do by building up your confidence that you can do it.

One way to build up your confidence for a task is to call on your Guide Dog from time to time during the day to remind you that you can and will do it. To do so, take a few quiet minutes now and then to get calm and centered. Then, imagine that your Guide Dog is telling you again and again: "You do can do it (fill in the image of whatever you want to do). You can do it."

Next, turn this into an "I" statement and by saying to yourself: "I can do it. I am doing it (fill in the image of yourself doing it)." At the same time, feel the support and confidence of your Guide Dog.

Then, see yourself doing what you want now, so your inner mind gets used to your doing it. Also, feel a sense of assurance and confidence that you are participating in this activity correctly and effectively.

You might additionally visualize others being pleased and complimenting you on whatever you have done (such as writing a good report, giving a good presentation, leading a successful meeting).

After this exercise, you'll feel better immediately. You'll be calmer, more relaxed, less worried about whatever you have to do. In addition, when it comes time to perform the activity, you'll do it better, because you feel more confident and have practiced doing it in your mind.

Increase Your Energy and Feel Less Tired

Calling on your dogs can help you get a quick charge or recharge of energy, such as if you feel sleepy or drowsy, have to start a big project that seems overwhelming, or need a rush to get you going in the morning and keep you going at night. These techniques work because you are using an image of a high-energy dog to give you the energy you need – whether one of your Power Dogs, your Top Dog, or a Rescue Dog you call on for the occasion. This kind of energy charge can often substitute for using anything artificial, like a pep pill, since you are drawing the needed energy from inside you, with the help of your dogs. The process works much like other types of energy techniques, using visualizations, except here you are using the visualization with some help from your dogs, as in the following two techniques.

Creating Your Own Energy and Enthusiasm

This is a technique to create a quick burst of energy and enthusiasm at any time, with a little dogged help. First, visualize or think of a fast, high energy dog.

Then, with this dog's image in mind, stand with your feet slightly apart and make a fist with one hand. Then, see this dog running rapidly either in a race or chasing a very fast animal, such as a rabbit. You see it going faster and faster, with mounting excitement in your mind's eye.

Now, as you see this dog running, quickly raise your hand to your head and lower it several times. Each time you bring it down, shout out something like: "I am awake," "I feel energetic," "I am enthusiastic and excited," or "I am raring to get up and go."

Repeat this five to ten times, and each time feel a rush of energy and enthusiasm surge through you. Soon you'll be awake and alert and ready to tackle any project. In fact, after you have repeatedly practiced this exercise, you can simply imagine this dog racing or chasing something and your energy and enthusiasm will increase, because of the power of repeated association.

Ideally, do this exercise initially in reality, since it's more stimulating to use your whole body. But if other people are around, so you can't actively participate without seeming strange or disruptive, imagine yourself doing this exercise in your mind's eye. Then, your mental imagery or self-talk can help to wake you up or motivate you to act. Eventually, the whole process will become a habit so just thinking of a dog racing or chasing will be enough to energize you.

Drawing on the Energies of the Universe

In this technique, which Gini adapted from a technique she first described in *Mind Power,* you get a little help from your dogs to make the experience even more vivid. You imagine that you have columns of energy flowing into and through you, with one stream of energy coming up from the earth and the other from the air. Meanwhile, one of your Power Dogs, Top Dog, or an especially strong Rescue Dog is seated beside you, helping to gather this energy. For example, visualize the dog digging in the ground to unleash the earth energy that pours into you, and then see him facing the wind to draw the energy of the air toward you. As you feel these two streams of energy pour into you, you feel energized – and this process has real biological effects, since it stimulates the molecules of energy in your body to move more quickly, so you both feel and become more energetic.

As these two types of energy pour into your body, notice they are slightly different. Notice that the earth energy that pours into your feet and surges up through your body feels very strong, giving you increased energy and power. Meanwhile, the air energy that streams in through the top of your head and down into your body feels light, airy, and expansive, giving you a sense of buoyancy.

Next, focus on the two energies meeting at the base of your spine, and see them join and spiral around together. Then they move up and down your spine and fill you with energy. You can balance the two energies, if you wish, by drawing on extra energy from the earth (heavy) or from the universe (light) as you wish. Meanwhile, your dog is outside, helping to direct more and more energy to you.

Keep running this energy up and down your spine until you feel filled with energy. Then, if you have a project or task you want to do, direct this energy toward doing this project. Even if you haven't felt especially motivated and enthused to do this task, you will feel this increased energy and enthusiasm to work on this project now, and you will feel increased confidence knowing you can do it with all this extra energy.

Whatever the project is, as you go to tackle it, feel this energy pouring from you into the project, while your dog sends you even more energy. It's like the dog you called on to help is acting like a pump, drawing the energy from the earth and the air and directing it to you, so you experience it energizing and can direct that energy into whatever task you want to do.

For example, if you want to write or type something, visualize the energy surging out through your hands. If you plan to lift some heavy objects, visualize the energy coming out through your feet, body, and arms. If you are going to teach a class or sell something, see the energy pouring into your voice as you speak. Or just see this energy pour into you as you start the day.

Both these and the previous techniques are great energy builders. But they're not designed to replace the sleep you need. Think of them more like quick energy-fixers to be used on a short-term basis. Should you keep drifting off while doing something or find yourself continually tired, after using these exercises, get more sleep.

Increase Your Feelings of Confidence and Self-Esteem

You can build up your feelings of confidence and self-esteem with the help of your Power Dogs, Top Dog, and Rescue Dogs, too, to better get what you want in life. Even if you haven't done something before, being confident, can help you do it; it can help you get better at something more quickly, because you are more focused and sure of yourself as you practice. And, when you feel more confident, you don't let any negative criticisms get you down; you don't take them personally, because you feel certain you can deal with the problem and overcome it. You are confident you can do better, and so you will.

This approach works because *if you believe you are great, you are great!* Then, that belief helps to create the experiences you have that support this belief. For example, if you are convinced you should have a certain job or promotion, you'll exude an aura of confidence and act like you belong in that job, so people will think of you in that role. Plus, with that belief, you'll know you can do whatever is required and will be able to do it. And you will have that ability because you believe you can and confidently do what is necessary to turn your belief into a reality.

Where do your dogs come in? In several ways. Your Guide Dogs can help you as you think about your good qualities that help build your esteem. Your Power Dogs can give you support and increase your feelings of confidence about your abilities, skills, and likelihood of success as you engage in activities. And, as needed, a Rescue Dog can provide you with even more confidence to build you up. Here are some key techniques to use to build confidence.

Acknowledge your Good Qualities, Talents, and Accomplishments

You gain confidence in yourself and what you can do by acknowledging your good qualities, talents, and accomplishments. Here's where your Guide Dogs can be especially helpful in identifying what these attributes are and helping you concentrate on them to remind yourself how great you are.

One way to do this exercise is to find a place where you can quietly think about what you like about yourself and what you have done well. Before you start, imagine that one or more of your Guide Dogs are with you. Though you can think about your qualities, talents, and accomplishments on your own, your Guide Dog adds additional support as you think about these qualities. Also, sometimes people are hesitant to praise themselves, thinking this seems too prideful or boastful. But if you have someone else, such as a friend or in this case your Guide Dog praising you to the skies, that's okay.

So now get started thinking about all your good qualities. To do so, get a sheet of paper and a pencil, divide the paper into three columns, and head each one: "My Good Qualities", "What I Can Do Well", and "What I Have Accomplished". It should look something like this:

	What Are My Good Qualities?	**What I Can Do Well?**	**What Are My Biggest Accomplishments?**
1			
2			
3			
4			
Etc.			

With this paper in front of you, get very relaxed, and imagine your Guide Dog is sitting beside you giving you answers. Ask your Guide Dog the question at the head of each column and listen to the answers. Then, as quickly as you can, write down whatever your Guide Dog says. When you start to slow down, repeat the question again, listen and write some more. Conclude by asking: "Anything else?" write down these last items, and go on to the next heading.

After you are finished, review your list. As you read each item, see yourself with that quality, talent, or accomplishment, and feel your Guide Dog praising you, telling you how "Great" and "Wonderful" you are. Experience how good it feels to get this praise. Finally, see your Guide Dog giving you a large blue "Best of Show" ribbon – just like a judge might give a show dog a ribbon. Then, pat yourself on the back to congratulate yourself and hear your Guide Dog barking out his or her excited approval, too.

Affirm Yourself and All Your Talents and Abilities

Affirmations are another great way to build confidence and self-esteem by asserting that you already have the qualities you want to develop. You keep making these affirmations as you work on developing these qualities with even more confidence.

This approach works because you are what you think. So if you think positively you'll feel positively. And if you think you have certain qualities and talents, that's how you'll be. Even if you don't have these characteristics now, by thinking you have them, you'll develop them and your self-esteem will soar.

In this case, your Power Dogs can contribute to the process by being there as your cheerleaders, making these affirmations that much stronger. So imagine one or more of your Power Dogs by your side as you do this exercise, and experience them cheering for you as you say each affirmation. Should you want help in deciding what your affirmations should be, call on one of your Guide Dogs to help you create your affirmations.

Take a sheet of paper, write down an appropriate header (i.e.: "Who I Am Now"), and begin writing down your affirmations about who you are, want to be, or what you have or want. Choose whatever is most important to you, and affirm it in the present tense, even if you don't have that thing or quality now. Use the present tense, because we become the way we see ourselves now. You can ask your Guide Dog for help with what to write or for additional ideas.

For example, you might affirm that:
I have an exciting, interesting job I really enjoy.
I have gotten that new job I want and I enjoy my new office.
I am a dynamic speaker and can keep an audience excited about what I say.
I have met the partner I want and we are getting married in a gala celebration.
Etc.

After you finish writing, select your most important affirmation and focus on it for about a minute. Close your eyes if you prefer. Repeat your affirmation over and over to yourself aloud or mentally, and as you do, see yourself in this imagined situation. Don't just say the words, but see yourself there. At the same time, as you engage in this activity, see your Power Dog eagerly jumping up and down or barking, giving you its strength and support.

Do this technique daily for about a week, and you'll notice that you feel more confident and that the things you want will start coming into your life. These affirmations work, because this mental and visual reinforcement helps to change your attitude about yourself, so you not only see yourself in a different way, but you feel better and therefore more confident about yourself, too. Then, your changed self-image will lead others to perceive and respond to you differently, because they can sense this air of increased confidence – much like you can stare down a dog that might be ready to attack. When you look like you are confident and sure of yourself, typically, the dog will sense that strength coming from you and back off, not wanting to challenge you.

Visualize Yourself as a Successful Person Achieving a Goal or Having Everything You Want

Seeing yourself as a success in achieving a goal, having what you want, or being recognized for your accomplishments can increase your confidence, too, since success builds self-esteem. So does visualizing yourself as successful. You see that desired vision as a reality, which helps you feel more self-assured. You feel more powerful, dynamic, and recognized, and these positive feelings contribute to your being more confident.

Here your Guide Dog can help you decide what you most want, and your Power Dog can give you more strength, as you imagine you now have what you want in the here and now. Once you decide to do this technique, repeat it regularly for several days to reinforce this success image and strengthen your feelings of self-esteem. Later, turn these feelings into reality by initiating new actions for success or responding confidently to new opportunities, knowing you have the ability to achieve them.

To start the process, decide what type of goal is most important to you in your work or personal life. To help with this process, you can imagine your Guide Dog is beside you. Then, ask the question: "What goal do I most want to achieve now?" and listen for the answer. Should several goals come to mind, pick the one that feels the most important to work on now.

Next, get relaxed, close your eyes, and see yourself realizing this goal. Make your image of this achievement as vivid as possible, and see your success happening in the here and now. Meanwhile, as you see this image appear in your mind's eye, imagine that your Power Dog is seated beside you, happily watching and cheering you on. It may be jumping up and down, barking happily, wagging its tail excitedly, or otherwise showing enthusiasm and support.

As you visualize your success, experience the feeling of satisfaction and power this brings. Feel elated, excited, strong, powerful, fully self-confident, and in charge. See others come over to you or call to congratulate you. You feel warm and glowing as you receive their praise. They tell you how successful you are. And you feel wonderful, able to do anything you want.

Set and Achieve Goals

You can also call on your dogs to help with setting and achieving your goals. Their primary role is to help you make choices when you use various goal-setting techniques. Essentially, you ask your questions, and your Guide Dogs help you answer them, sometimes more honestly, since calling on them helps you tap into your unconscious desires and needs. Your dogs can also help you establish more specific and realistic goals and set priorities, which are critical for reaching your goals. If you are too vague, don't feel an intense conviction that you really want something, and don't prioritize, you diffuse your energy by going after too many things simultaneously, rather than focusing on what you want the most.

In short, to get what you want, do the following:
1. Have a clear specific picture of what you want
2. Prioritize your most important goals.

3. Focus on your more important goals first — at most, two or three at a time.
4. Make sure each goal is realistically achievable.
5. Infuse your goal with a determined conviction that you really want it and are willing to do what it takes to get it.

These are fairly basic goal-setting principles. The following techniques can help you better set and achieve these goals by calling on your Power Dogs or Top Dog for help.

Getting a Clear Specific Picture of What You Want and Prioritizing What to Do

This technique will help you focus on what you really want and set your priorities by using visualization or self-talk, combined with automatic writing, to record your answers. The process helps you get at what you really think and feel by letting go of your conscious mind, so your thoughts flow more spontaneously.

Get prepared by taking a sheet of paper and writing down the questions you want answered, such as, "What Do I Want to Gain or Achieve?", "Why is This Goal Important to Me Now?", "What is My Most Important Goal or Goals?", "How Realistic is This Goal?"

Your sheet of paper will look something like the following table:

What Do I Want to Gain or Achieve?	Why is This Goal Important to Me Now?	What is My Most Important Goal or Goals?	How Realistic is This Goal?

Then, get very relaxed and imagine one of your Guide Dogs (or your Top Dog) sitting across from you. Your dog is there, eager to listen and help you first determine your goals and prioritize your most important goal or goals. Later, you can ask your dog what you need to do to get there.

Now start asking your questions. Don't try to guide the answer yourself. Instead, let your Guide Dog (or Top Dog) answer. And write down whatever comes to you.

First ask, "What do I want to gain or achieve?" and list whatever answers you get. Then, for each goal, asking "Why is this goal important to me now?" and record your answers. As you look at these different goals, ask your Guide (or Top) Dog: "What goal or goals are most important to me now?" or "Which goal or goal should I concentrate on achieving first?" Then, note the first of the three goals that come to mind.

For those goals you have listed, ask: "How realistic is achieving this goal?" and ask your Guide (or Top) Dog to give you one of three answers: "Realistic", "Maybe", or "Pipedream". Then, write that down. If you get any pipedreams, eliminate that goal, and concentrate on the others. Should you get all pipedreams, you have a problem setting realistic goals and should look at the other goals you have listed to determine which are most important to do now. Or if you have no more goals listed, start the exercise again, and this time ask your Guide or Top Dog to only suggest goals you can really accomplish.

Once you have selected one to three goals, these are the goals to concentrate on achieving first.

Developing the Conviction and Confidence to Achieve Your Goals

Once you are clear what you want, know your goals are realistic, and are certain this is your most important goal or goals, put your energy and determination into achieving each goal and regularly re-affirm this conviction. This way, you continue to re-energize that goal and remind yourself that you will achieve it and will do what is necessary to do so.

Your Power Dog can help, as a supporter and cheerleader adding its power to increase your conviction and confidence. Here's how.

Get relaxed and close your eyes. Find a few minutes during the day, or do this exercise as you drift off to sleep or right after you wake up.

Imagine your Power Dog is sitting beside you and concentrate all your attention on realizing your goal. See your goal already achieved, whether it's a material possession, job, desired relationship, or new home. And see your Power Dog in the scene with you. Make the images of your goal as clear as possible and be aware of everything you see — colors, objects, people, rooms, furnishings, and so on. Listen to what you hear around you — sounds, voices, conversations. Touch objects around you. Notice anything you smell, taste, or sense moving. And see your Power Dog walking around, looking, listening, and lending you its power and support. In short, experience achieving your goal as fully as possible.

As you see this goal achieved, very vividly, say to yourself: "I will achieve this goal. I will do what is necessary to get it. This goal is completely possible. I just need to act to get it, and it will happen now!"

Finally, end the visualization and return to normal consciousness feeling fully convinced and certain you will get what you want. This feeling will stay with you during the day and will help you take the necessary steps to achieve your goal.

Determining the Steps to Achieve Your Goal

Once you set your goal and have the conviction and determination to achieve it, the next step is breaking it down into specific objectives or steps to accomplish including noting what resources you might need along the way. You also need to work out the sequence of what you will do when. Essentially, this is basic "Goal-setting and Achieving 101", which is much like setting out the steps for designing a project. After you determine these steps, the final stage is implementation – where you put your plan into action and work toward your goal. Whole books are written about this process.

Again, you can call on your Guide or Top Dog to help you decide what you need to do, the resources you require, and how to order and prioritize these activities, so you can carry out your action plan most efficiently. The role of your Guide Dog or Top Dog is to help you get into a frame of mind to see things in a holistic, intuitive way and thereby streamline the goal planning process.

To prepare, get a sheet of paper and a pencil and write the goal you want to accomplish on top. Next make four columns entitled: What I Need to Do, Resources I Need, Order of Execution, and Importance of Activity. Your paper will look something like this:

What I Need to Do	Resources I Need	Order of Execution	Importance of Activity

Then, with this paper before you, get relaxed and imagine your Guide Dog or Top Dog is seated in front of you, eager to help by answering your questions. Once you feel completely relaxed and in a meditative frame of mind, ask your Guide Dog or Top Dog: "What are all the things I need to do to reach my goal?" Don't try to guide the process or judge how important these activities are now. Just write down everything that comes to you in the first column. Keep asking this question and writing down your ideas until you feel finished. The process is like brainstorming, using your Guide Dog or Top Dog to help limber up the process, so you are even more receptive and creative than usual.

Next go to the second column and ask your Guide Dog or Top Dog the following question for each item you have listed in the first column: "What resources do I need to do these activities?" Write down whatever answers you receive. Again, don't try to guide the process or judge or evaluate your thoughts. Just write down whatever resources your Guide Dog or Top Dog tells you. Keep going until you feel finished for each item — and if you don't need anything special for a particular activity, go on to the next.

Now go to the third column and ask your Guide Dog or Top Dog this question to help you order the activities listed in Column 1: "What should I do first? What should I do next? And so on." Number these items accordingly. If you are not sure of the order or feel you will do some activities around the same time, give them the same number.

Finally, go to the last column and ask your Guide Dog or Top Dog to help you prioritize these activities, so if you don't have time to do everything, you can drop the less important activities. Ask: "What is the importance of this activity?" and for each one, ask your Guide Dog or Top Dog to rate these with an "A" for most important, "B" for next most important, and "C" for least important to only do if possible. Again, don't try to guide this process. Just listen as your Guide Dog or Top Dog tells you the ranking.

When you are done, return to your everyday state of consciousness. Now take the information you have acquired to make up an activities list for yourself. List the goal you are going to achieve at the top of the page, and using the numbers listed in column 3, write down the activities you plan to do and the resources you need to do them. Next to each one, write the letter indicating the importance of this activity.

Your sheet of paper will look something like this:

Goal #	Goal	Resources Needed	Priority

Putting Your Goal into Action

Once you know your goal, are committed to achieving it, and know what to do to get it, the final step is to START NOW! Here your Power Dog can help by giving you additional energy, power, and support – or a Rescue Dog might join in as well. The more the merrier, as they say.

This final phase is where you might also use the energy raising techniques in this chapter to infuse you with more energy to get started with enthusiasm. Then, too, you can use some of the confidence and esteem-building techniques to increase your self-assurance that you will attain your goal.

With this conviction, commitment and focused energy, begin the process of going after and getting what you want. As you do, imagine your Power Dogs (and maybe a Rescue Dog if needed) are right beside or just behind you, giving you their energy and support.

As you see yourself moving toward your goal, know you'll get it. Believe you can do it. Do what is necessary to accomplish your goal. And you will! Just thinking, imagining, and knowing what you want and directing your energy and enthusiasm toward your goal will mobilize you to take the appropriate actions to get it.

So send in the dogs and go for it! Use the power of your imagination to call on your dogs to give you even more power.

Perhaps a way to think of this process is like driving a dog sled, with a team of very powerful dogs pouring their energy into pulling that sled ever faster and faster until you achieve your goal. You draw on their power and you get there.

So go to it with enthusiasm and confidence. Get going! Do it now! Mush!!!

An Example of How to Use the System

How does the system work in practice? Here's an example.

Take Robert who wants to move into a management job with more responsibility, but he feels cowed by a fellow co-worker, Jim, who is an outgoing go-getter. Jim often gets others to cover for him at the home office, while he is out schmoozing with people and bringing in clients, so he's a natural charismatic fundraiser and it looks like he will get the management nod.

But Robert is much better in managing details in his own quiet way, if only the top executives knew this. Yet Robert feels uncertain about what to do, afraid he won't be able to show off his strengths, and worse, he believes if he says anything to compare himself to Jim, the attempt will backfire, and he could even be out of a job. Thus, he feels highly anxious, lacks confidence, and is unclear about any next steps to take.

Here's how he might use the Dog Type system.

First, since he needs to calm down, he starts with a relaxing visualization. However because the office is usually very busy and noisy, he waits until he gets home, leans back on the recliner in the living room, and turns down the lights. Then, with some soft music playing in the background, he calls on a Rescue Dog to help him relax and feel less anxious. At once the image of a Golden Retriever pops into his mind. So he invites the Retriever to join him as he thinks of a fun, enjoyable activity.

In moments, he recalls how he loves to go to the beach and walk along the sand dunes, and he sees himself walking with this Golden Retriever, he names Sam. As they walk, he concentrates on being fully in the moment, and experiences the waves lapping softly on the beach, as the tide washes in and out. He enjoys the warm sun, while smelling the salty air, and seeing the gently rolling dunes. Meanwhile, he hears Sam saying: "Relax. Relax," as they walk. When he opens his eyes, he feels much calmer, and ready to move on to going after what he really wants.

His next step is to do a little confidence building, since he feels he has the skills and ability, but has trouble showing this to others. So he takes some time to reflect on his good qualities and remind himself of what he does well. Again he sits down on his recliner, this time with a pad and paper, and he begins imagine that his very sensitive, intelligent Poodle, Cheri, is with him as a Guide Dog to answer his questions.

Then, focusing on his desired management job, he uses self-talk to mentally ask Cheri his questions. "What good qualities do I have for this job?" "What tasks can I do well?" "What are my strongest accomplishments at work?" After he asks each question, he holds his pencil poised, ready to write as Cheri responds, telling him about his major strengths. "You have a great sense of loyalty…You're always on time…People can really count on you…People trust you…You are well organized…You are thoughtful…You did a great job leading your team to complete a project…"And so the questions continue until Cheri runs out of answers for him.

Later, as he reviews his lists, seeing himself with each quality or recalling how he completed these tasks, he sees Cheri by his side listening intently. From time to time, she barks her approval or tells him: "You really did a great job" or "You really are good at that." He concludes by seeing Cheri lift up her paw, with a big blue ribbon hanging from it. He grabs the ribbon, holds it, and feels really good, that he really deserves this reward.

Then, as he imagines himself holding the ribbon, he repeats some affirmations to himself: "I have very good management skills," "People in the office really like me," "I'm a great organizer," and he will repeat those affirmations to himself during the week, as a further reinforcement of his abilities.

Finally, after a brief break for dinner, he returns to do some goal setting and planning. This time, after he gets relaxed in his lounge chair and again visualizes Cheri beside him, he asks the question: "What goal do I most want to achieve now?" and he gets the reassurance that yes, he does want to go after the management goal. So he focuses on seeing himself in this new position. He imagines himself in his new office talking to employees, and giving them help and guidance when they have questions about what to do. He visualizes telling his supervisor how much he and his team have accomplished. He also sees Jim, the go-getter, reporting to him and doing an even better job at racking up sales and bringing in new clients, because he's really good at that. Then, he sees himself praising Jim, telling him what a great job he has done, so Jim will keep doing what he has been doing best and get even better.

After that, he asks Cheri to help him decide what to do next to achieve that goal. The answer comes back loud and clear – you need to show your boss you are up to the job, ready to do it, and have a plan about what to do. So, later that night, Robert writes his thoughts into a management plan, suggesting ways to make the office even more productive and how to reward Jim as the office's top producer. As Robert writes, he imagines Bull, his Bullmastiff Power Dog nearby cheering him on, and when he finishes, he takes a few minutes to imagine how he will present himself and his ideas to his boss.

This time he imagines a scenario where he confidently calls up his boss, tells him he's got some ideas for increasing office productivity, and would like to meet with him to share his ideas. As he calls, he imagines Bull right beside him, giving him more power and self-assurance.

Then, in reality, when Robert actually does call up his boss, he feels the strength and confidence he has built up as he asks for the meeting. He even imagines that Cheri and Bull are hovering nearby, lending their strength and support. Finally, when he goes into the meeting, he has that new confidence and assurance as a result of processes he has used to get rid of his anxiety, increase his confidence, be clear about his goal, and know what to do to get it.

The result? Robert shows his boss he really does have the ability and vision to do the job, as well as the confidence to show he is the best person to do it. And so he gets the promotion and new job.

Similarly, other people might use and adapt these techniques for their own purposes – from the workplace to their personal life – to relax, increase energy, build confidence, and set and achieve goals.

You'll see some examples of other ways to use these techniques in the next chapter.

CHAPTER 2: OTHER WAYS OF USING THE DOG TYPE SYSTEM

As you become familiar with using the Dog Type system, you will find more and more ways to use it in everyday life. You may even get a dog if you don't already have one – and your choice of Top Dog, Watch Dog, Guide Dog, Power Dogs, and Rescue Dogs may help you decide what kind of dog to get.

Besides the methods described in previous chapters, other ways of applying the system include: increasing your skills and creativity, solving problems and making decisions, simply having fun, and techniques featured in this chapter. Plus you can use these techniques for virtually any other type of self-help and relationship assistance. Simply call on your different types of dogs to assist.

Increase Your Skills

As researchers have discovered, using mental imagery can help improve your performance, whether you're rehearsing a speech or performing athletic gymnastics in your mind. Over the past few decades, millions of people have used this widely accepted practice to develop and perfect their skills. The process works by enabling you to practice or rehearse a skill in your mind to supplement your real practice, so you get better at it. You see yourself hitting that tennis serve perfectly; you see yourself in front of an audience of thousands giving a great speech; you imagine yourself typing a letter at your computer and get faster and faster.

Through this mental practice and rehearsal, you reinforce what you have learned through physical practice, since the mind doesn't clearly distinguish between what you do mentally and in reality. The result is that you lay down these neural pathways which are like macros on the computer. You launch them to play for you when you engage in this skill, so you cut down on actual practice time and speed up the time you need to improve.

Furthermore, when you work with the skill you want to acquire in your mind, you can see yourself performing it perfectly, thereby providing an ideal model to achieve when you perform the activity in reality. But you need to do it correctly in your mind for this to work. Otherwise, your mental mistakes will translate into real world ones. Thus, be sure to know in advance the ideal way to perform this skill (such as watching an expert play a good game of tennis; listening to an expert speaker give a speech), so you have a role model in mind when you practice mentally. Or initially visualize yourself using a method you have learned to do physically.

However you learn this ideal method for performing this skill, see yourself doing it correctly and effectively, as your mental image will eventually translate into reality. Also, imagine yourself practicing the skills you desire as vividly as possible. Visualize the setting; see yourself or others dressed appropriately to practice that skill; notice others in the environment. The more real you can make your mental experience, the more powerful it will be in translating into a real life event.

Just as you get better at a skill in reality through repeated practice, so you should repeat this visualization again and again, to give it more power. As you practice, feel yourself becoming more skilled, confident, and assured, and this feeling will carry over into real time and will help you perform better.

The way the Dog Type system works with this process in that you call on your dogs to help you get even better at perfecting a skill. They do so by acting as advisers, supporters, and cheerleaders to give you even more power and confidence as you engage in these skill visualizations. They also make these visualizations more vivid and intense, and therefore, more powerful.

Use the following visualization to practice with the help of your chosen dog or dogs.

Close your eyes and get very relaxed. Imagine that your Top Dog, Power Dog, Guide Dog, or any other dog you feel can help is there with you to give you advice and support.

Then, see yourself participating in whatever skill you want to practice. You can practice by yourself, or you can see people in the audience watching you if this is a skill you perform in front of a group or crowd.

Now, whether you are practicing alone or in front of a group, you see your chosen dog helping you by your side or in the stands cheering you on. If you are practicing this skill for the first time, ask your Guide Dog for advice on exactly how to do it. As you get ready to perform, listen to his suggestions about what to do, such as how and where to stand, how to move, or whatever you need to do.

Then, as you perform the skill, your Top Dog, Power Dog, or any other dog you want there, are enthusiastically cheering you on. Each time you complete an activity, they call out their praise with cheers or barks, and show their excitement for how well you are doing. They may jump up and down, clap their paws together, wag their tail energetically. And you feel that enthusiasm, giving you even more assurance and confidence as you continue to perform that skill perfectly well.

Finally, after you have repeated this practice for several minutes, stop practicing, and take a bow to your Top Dog, Power Dog, or any other audience that has been watching. Then, come back into present reality.

You'll find that this mental practice, particularly when you repeat it for several days, will soon translate into an improved performance. Continue doing this visualization until you have acquired the facility you want with that skill. Once you attain this level, if you continue to perform this skill regularly, your everyday habit reflexes will take over. As a result, soon you'll be able to perform this skill automatically and effectively, whether you practice mentally or not, and you won't need to practice mentally on a regular basis.

However, from time to time, to polish your abilities, go over your skill in your mind, and as before, imagine that your Top Dog, Power Dog, or other dogs you want to invite are watching you and enthusiastically praising your performance. If you expect to use these skills for a particularly critical occasion, such as a sports competition or speech to an important group, mentally review, so you feel completely prepared and psyched up to put on your best possible performance.

Increase Your Creativity

You can call on your dogs to up your creativity, too. Just using this system is an exercise in being creative, because you are developing your powers to visualize and tap into your intuition, which are at the heart of creativity. Through your creative visuals, you're envisioning all sorts of things – from goals to achieve to new ways to organize an organization or your life.

The essence of creativity is coming up with new ideas, doing things differently, thinking of alternative approaches, and seeing things in new ways. In today's world of continual change and transformation, creativity is especially important, because you have to continually adapt and even remake yourself to take on new roles in new situations with new people. By increasing your creativity, you increase your ability to change and adapt.

There are all sorts of ways to increase your creativity, which Gini has written about in *Mind Power, The Empowered Mind,* and *The Intuitive Edge.* The Dog Type system is still another way to increase your ability to come up with new ideas and direct your creative processes so they are more effective and productive. Calling on your dogs is a way to build on other systems for developing creativity by using them for advice, support, and intensifying the experience, so you become even more creative.

The following techniques will to help you increase your creativity by further developing the qualities and attitudes that make up creativity, such as:
- seeing new ways of doing things,
- perceiving and thinking in innovative ways,
- being open to alternative ways of doing things.

As you develop these qualities and attitudes, you can apply this outlook to any area you choose to express your creativity. These possibilities are endless, ranging from being innovative in how you dress or design your room to coming up with ideas for new products, programs, and organizational systems at work.

The following techniques illustrate three ways to be creative and call on your dogs to further increase your creativity in the workplace and in your personal life. As you work with these techniques, you'll limber up your brain to think and perceive in new ways, which enables you to apply your creativity in multiple areas of your life, since your creative abilities can easily be adapted from one sphere of activity to another.

Seeing New Uses for Things

The advantage of coming up with new uses for things is you can maximize what something does. On a practical note, this is a good way to increase the value of something or reduce expenses, because you have more uses for the same thing. For example, besides reading a book, you can use it to make measurements when you don't have a ruler, or use it for a weight to press flowers.

This technique will get you thinking about new uses for things – with a little help from your Guide Dog. You begin by imagining new uses for familiar items as a warm up to attune your brain for quickly sliding from one idea to another. Then, you apply the process to a specific situation, say at work, where you want to discover new uses for things. So get ready, get relaxed, and go, using the following exercise.

First, see how many new and unusual uses you can come up with for a series of familiar objects. Begin by getting some paper and a pencil. As you hold the paper, imagine that your Guide Dog is beside you, ready to give you ideas.

Divide each page into three or four columns, and write down the name of one familiar object in each column. To come up with objects, look around your office or house and write down the names of objects your see. Or turn to your Guide Dog and ask: "What are some familiar objects I can use?" Then, listen to the answers and write them down, one per column.

Now, look at the name of each object in turn, and as you do, mentally ask this question to your Guide Dog: "What are all the uses you can think of for this object?" Then, listen and write as quickly as you can. As soon as the suggestions for uses stop flowing, ask your Guide Dog again: "What other uses can you think of?" Again, listen and write as quickly as possible. When the process slows again, go to the next object.

Seek to make these uses as novel as possible, and feel free to change the size, shape, or color of the object to do so. You can also combine this object with other objects. Invite your Guide Dog to come up with ideas reflecting these changes and combinations.

When you feel warmed up, think about any situations in your life in which you might want to apply this technique. If you aren't sure which situation to use, ask your Guide Dog: "What situation in my life would I like to change?" Then, listen to what your Guide Dog says, without trying to guide the process.

For example, if your company is marketing a new product, think of all the possible uses for it, or think of all the ways the company might advertise it. Or, say you are planning a party. Think of all the things you might do to make this a unique experience for everyone.

Finding New Methods or Materials to Achieve a Goal

Another way to increase your creativity is coming up with alternate methods or discover different resources that enable you to reach a goal – whether it's a goal at work (like completing a task or launching a product) or in your personal life (like all the ways you can amuse the relatives when they come to visit).

The process of finding new methods or materials can apply to anything. Just think "I can do it," and think of all the ways you can accomplish that task and what you need to accomplish it. You may be able to use what you already have although in new ways. Or maybe you need to get other resources and come up with creative ways to get them.

For instance, suppose you have to get across town and you discover the road you usually take is blocked. Maybe there is another route across unfamiliar roads you can take in your car. Or maybe it would be better not to go by car at all. Maybe you would do better taking a bike. Or maybe you don't need to take the trip now and can go another day. Or maybe…maybe… In other words, you may come up with all sorts of alternate ways to achieve that goal or even change the goal to something else.

Again, your Guide Dog can assist by helping you come up with all sorts of creative suggestions – more than you might think of yourself – helping you to tap more deeply into your intuitive and unconscious thinking.

Use the following guidelines to help loosen up your thinking processes to better come up with new approaches to achieve your goals. As before, first work with the technique to limber up your mind; then apply it to a particular goal you want to achieve.

First, get a sheet of paper and pencil, get relaxed, and imagine your Guide Dog is seated in front of you, eager to come up with ideas for you.

Now think of how many ways you can come up with to fill a need or achieve a goal. Start with some simple needs or goals to practice the process. For example, use a goal such as: "to plan a great party...to take a unique trip...to get across town faster...to keep burglars away." Should you need help thinking of what goals to use, ask your Guide Dog, and listen for the answers and write them down.

Next, look at each activity individually, imagine you have unlimited resources to create solutions, and start brainstorming. To do so, ask your Guide Dog: "How many new approaches can you think of to reach this goal?" Then, let the answers come as quickly as possible. Don't try to critique them or explain them. Just write them down. If your Guide Dog slows down, ask the question: "What other new approaches can you think of to reach this goal?" Then, listen uncritically and write down whatever your Guide Dog tells you.

Later, you can evaluate these ideas and think about which ones you might choose if you were going to do so.

Once you are comfortable using this process, apply it to a real situation where you want to come up with ideas. Afterward, you can assess these ideas, rate them based on how much you would like to use them, and finally choose any ideas you can use to implement in the future.

Changing What Already Exists – or Finding New Combinations

A third key creativity method is changing what already exists in different ways or finding new ways to combine and recombine what already exists. Such a change can contribute to keeping people stimulated and enthusiastic at work or in a relationship. It prevents boredom and keeps motivation high. Those in the entertainment business know the power of creative change, so they are always looking for something new to keep people entertained. They don't just follow "the show must go on!"

motto, but the adage, "The NEW show must be developed to keep going." And, those in the high-tech industry are continually looking for the next new thing.

Likewise, you can use this creative change approach to improve your life at work and in your personal life. For example, change the décor or your fashion to add more excitement to your life. Reorganize the way you do things in the office to promote efficiency and improve motivation. Or if you're on a tight budget, find ways to create some inexpensive furniture, such as by turning a pile of colorful cushions into a comfortable couch.

Use the following exercises to help you think change, and as before, invite your Guide Dog to sit in front of you and help you brainstorm ideas. After you practice limbering up your brain power in this way, you can apply this process to specific situations where real change would be useful.

To start each exercise, get a sheet of paper, get relaxed, imagine your Guide Dog eagerly seated in front of you, and ask the question: "What are all the ways I can change..."You fill in the blanks. Just listen and write as your Guide Dog makes suggestions to you.

- Changing Things *(especially useful for developing new inventions, creating new products, devising new systems, etc.) See how many changes you can make in familiar objects. Imagine the different uses these objects might have when changed. Think of all the ways you can change each object — in size, color, style, construction. Don't expect every idea to be useful and practical. Rather, come up with as many ideas as you can as quickly as possible. Later you can go through these ideas and pick out those that might work.*

- Changing Places *(especially useful for changing landscaping and the look of your home or work environment). Discover how many changes you can make in what you see. Use a picture or look around you. To alter what you see, mentally add something, modify or rearrange things, change size relationships, or take something away. For example, add in flowers or pictures to a room; see different plants in a garden; imagine that a building on the street is no longer there. Don't feel your ideas have to be practical ones. Just let your mental processes flow and generate as many ideas as you can. Later, you can select out what's practical and make changes accordingly.*

- Changing People *(especially useful for changing your own look to better project the image you want or changing the way you interact with others.) Think of the many ways you can change people or yourself. While you can do this exercise wherever you are – say at a cocktail party or while waiting for a plane as people rush by, you can also visualize making these changes in your head. For example, ask your Guide Dog: "What would this person look like if..."Then, see the picture of this person change before you. For instance, suppose a man has a mustache or a beard. Ask your Guide Dog: "How would he look without it?" Or suppose a woman has long hair? Ask what she would look like if she had very short hair. Or take an elderly man? What might he look like if young? Keep going with other questions and be receptive to whatever comes to you. Later, you can apply this process to a real situation where you want to make changes, such as if you are thinking of changing your style to be more up-to-date or with it by wearing different clothes or adopting a new hair style.*

- Changing Your Interaction Style. *(especially useful for improving your relationships with others). Look at the different ways you can act and react in social situations. Imagine yourself in different situations, starting with a not very important setting so you get familiar with this technique, and see yourself acting and reacting in different ways, while your Guide Dog accompanies you, giving you tips on what to say or do and cheering you on. For example, see yourself going into a store and starting the conversation with a different opening remark. See yourself going up to someone you never met at a party and trying out different greetings. Imagine you are at a talk asking different questions. Once you get comfortable using this technique, try applying it to a real life situation that is important to you. When you do, note which approach gets a better response from others, and use that in real life to improve your interaction with that person.*

- Making New Combinations *(especially useful for inventing new products, creating new designs for your home or office, or reorganizing a group of people). Now you want to combine familiar objects or people to create unique arrangements. First practice the process by thinking of two or three familiar objects or people, and later apply this approach to practical situations. To begin, write down the names of the objects or people. Then, ask your Guide Dog to help you come up with suggestions, and in your mind's eye, see the objects or people on a stage in front of you. Make the setting as wild and fantastic as you want to inspire your creativity. You can make the objects or people larger or smaller than normal, too. The idea is to be as innovative and creative as you can. Later, you can apply your ideas to practical matters, because your ideas will come more quickly and freely.*

Solve Problems and Make Decisions

The Dog Type system can help you solve problems and make decisions, too, through brainstorming or using your intuition to know what to do.

The brainstorming process has become widely known, usually when done in a group. You can also do this very effectively as an individual, and for many people who are not comfortable sharing in a group setting, individual brainstorming is generally the most productive, creative way to come up with ideas. In either case, the goal of the brainstorming process is to first come up with as many alternative ideas or problem solutions as quickly as possible. Then, in the second phase of the process, the goal is to select the most appropriate ideas from this list and seek to implement them.

The brainstorming process is extremely effective at producing a variety of ideas, because you quickly generating whatever you think of without any restrictive attempts to evaluate them. That's why you need a two stage process, whether you do this individually or as a group — the first to generate ideas; the second to review them critically to eliminate unworkable ideas and prioritize those that are left.

Thus, the technique has become very popular not only for generating creative ideas, but for solving problems by coming up with a variety of alternative solutions. Such problems can be literally anything – from personal problems to problems at work.

Probably you are already familiar with some types of brainstorming. However, now you can call on your dogs, especially your Guide Dog, to help you brainstorm even more effectively. Generally, this process works best when you are brainstorming individually, since you can combine it with getting relaxed and visualizing. Besides, if other people aren't familiar with the Dog Type system, it may seem a little nutty to call on your dogs to help you brainstorm. (But as more and more people learn about the system and use it, sure, do this as a group...though, ummm, keep the barking down).

Here are two techniques using individual brainstorming, where you first generate as many ideas as possible, write them down, and then go over these ideas critically to select the best ones with the help of your Guide Dog. Here's how your Guide Dog can help at each phase of the two-step brainstorming process:

1) To further stimulate your imagination and intuition to think of as many ideas as possible, imagine your Guide Dog seated before you and ask him the question you are brainstorming. As in a usual brainstorming process, make the question clear, precise, and open-ended, such as: "What should I do about…?" or "What are some alternate solutions to…?" You fill in the blanks with the problem. Then, without trying to direct your Guide Dog, let him answer however he wants, listen to the answer, and, write it down.

2) To help you review these ideas to decide which are best for further development, ask your Guide Dog to sit beside you and help you rate these ideas to give you a quick assessment as you review each one. For example, ask for an "A" for the best ideas; "B" for the next best, and "C" for the next best after that. If any are clearly unsuitable, ask for an "X" to mark the spot. As an alternative, invite your Guide Dog to bark out his assessments – a loud enthusiastic bark or three barks for "great"; a regular bark or two barks for "good", a soft bark or one bark for "maybe", and a growl or no bark for "a definite no".

You can use this process to come up with alternative possibilities for just about anything from the smallest problem to complex long-term undertakings. The following technique will help you limber up your mental processes to start generating alternatives. Ideally, start with a less important or hypothetical problem to gain skill at using this process; then apply this technique to resolving an issue you are really concerned about.

Coming Up With Alternatives to Find Solutions

Start by writing down the problem you want to solve or objective you want to achieve on a sheet of paper. The problem or objective can be anything – a physical one such as building a house; an organizational one, such as resolving a personality clash between two people; or a personal matter, such as figuring out how to better get along with your mother-in-law. Next, divide your sheet of paper into three columns, headed approaches, persons, and objects. It will look something like this:

Problem I Want to Solve:		
Approaches	**Persons**	**Objects**

Now get very relaxed and imagine your Guide Dog is seated in front of you, eager to help, as in previous exercises.

For each column, ask your Guide Dog the following questions and listen to the answer. Don't try to guide the process. Just listen to what your Guide Dog says and write down whatever comes. Don't try to evaluate the comments either. Just listen and record.

The questions to ask for each of the columns are these:
- What are all the ways I can solve this problem?
- Who are the people or groups I need help from to make this happen?
- What are the objects I need to solve this problem?

Keep listening for answers as long as your Guide Dog has something to say. When the answers slow down or stop, ask this question: "Is there anything else you would suggest?" Again listen and write down whatever your Guide Dog says.

After you finish the three columns, review your list critically to determine which approaches are the best and which persons or items you really need. Ask your Guide Dog to give each one a "Yea" or "Nay" as good possibilities or not good at all using whatever method of communication you prefer (for example, he can tell you "Yea", bark, or wag his tail for a yes, or he can tell you "Nay," growl, or hold his tail down for "No".

After you've eliminated all the clearly bad ideas, rank the circled ideas in order of priority from "A" (highest priority) to "C" (lowest priority). You can ask your Guide Dog to help by telling you the rating as you go through each item on the list.

For practice, use this technique for simple or test problems. Then, apply it to more complex or real life problems in your work or personal life.

Use Your Intuition to Make Better Decisions

Besides coming up with alternatives and selecting the best one, another approach is using a more intuitive, holistic "ah-ha" method. Again you can get help from your Guide Dog to achieve this knowing ah-ha. This intuitive approach to making decisions is helpful when you have difficulty choosing among alternatives, or you don't have many alternatives, since your choice is basically "yes", "no", or deferring the decision to a later time when you are ready to decide. For instance, a limited alternative situation might be: Should you take the job offer or turn it down? Do you want to marry this person or not?

Sometimes it's hard to decide based on your reason alone, such as by weighing all the pros and cons to make your decision worse, using your logic can sometimes lead you to make a decision that makes rational sense, but you don't feel right about the result. By contrast, if you can tap directly into your unconscious or intuition, you can make that gut-level decision that expresses what you really want.

What if you have trouble hearing that inner intuitive voice? That's where your Guide Dog can help you tap into that inner response and pay attention to what it says to do.

The following techniques will help you do just that – connect with your inner self with a assistance from your Guide Dog. These techniques reflect different ways of making that connection: through automatic writing, visual symbols or thoughts or signals from your body. You call on your Guide Dog to help you experience and interpret these different forms of inner communication. Since different people get information in different ways and vary how they prefer to get it, these techniques provide alternate ways of getting this information. Try out these different methods; then choose the technique or techniques that work best for you in different situations.

<u>Getting a Quick Yes or No</u>

Here's a way to get a quick "Yes" or "No" to help you make a decision, when an extended visualization to find an answer will take too long, since you need an immediate decision. In this quickie approach, you see the words on a screen in your mind saying "Yes" or "No," or you hear a little voice telling you that. And to make the "Yes" or "No" even more clear and intense, call up a quick picture in your mind of your Guide Dog giving you the "Yes" sign (i.e.: smiling, wagging his tail) or the "No" sign (i.e.: lowering his head or tail) or you can hear your dog bark happily for "Yes" and growl or whine for "No". For a "Not sure", you can see your Guide Dog simply shake his head.

To program yourself to use the process, go through a list of questions where you already have a clear "Yes" or "No" answer, such as "Was I born in ____?" (your birth year); is my mother's name_____? And so on. As you answer, notice how you get the get the answer. You may see a "Yes" or "No" on the screen in your mind, or you may hear your inner voice say the answer. At the same time, use or hear your Guide Dog respond. However this response comes, concentrate on getting your future answers the same way, so you reinforce and validate that method of getting answers. Then, if both answers are the same, you can feel even more sure this is the correct answer for you. If not, take some time to assess your answers. The lack of consistency may suggest you aren't really sure. So it is better to wait before you make a decision and perhaps you might later do this exercise again, until your answers from two sources are the same and reassure you that your decision is now correct.

In first using this method, continue to ask yourself questions to which you know the answers and work on getting your response to come more quickly, until you hear or see it come like a flash, where you see or hear the "Yes" or "No" and your Guide Dog responding right away.

Initially, you will have to consciously call up this visualization, but gradually it will become a matter of habit, programmed into your mind. To make this happen, keep doing the process of answering "Yes" and "No" for several minutes, as you see and/or hear your Guide Dog respond appropriately.

Continue to practice this technique regularly for about a week and start using it to get answers for things where you really do want to know the answers as you go about your everyday life. You'll find that the process gradually becomes automatic. You'll find the "Yes", "No", or "Not sure" answers start popping up automatically on your mental screen along with your Guide Dog responding too, or you'll hear the answers spoken by your Guide Dog as your inner voice.

Keep using this technique every day, whenever you want to make a quick yes or no decision, and if you don't use it for a while, do a refresher to practice the technique, so it becomes automatic again.

Deciding the "Write" Way

The write way technique involves using automatic writing along with some input from your Guide Dog to help you decide. Start by having paper and pencil available or sit in front of your computer, so you can immediately begin to write. It also helps to set up a comfortable writing environment to help tap into your intuition, say by using candles or dim lighting. Then, get very relaxed and imagine your Guide Dog beside you, ready to give you suggestions.

Now ask your Guide Dog questions about your decision, such as "What should I do about_____?" "What is in my best interest to do about_____?" "What would I really like to do about_____?" You can also ask about options, such as asking: "What are my alternatives?" and "Which alternatives would I prefer?"

Then wait for your Guide Dog to answer. Don't try to guide the answers. Just be receptive, listen, and start writing as the answers come to you. Don't think or analyze. Just write. Keep asking questions and recording the answers until the questions and responses stop coming.

Finally, review what you have written. The course you want to take should be clear.

Asking Your Guide Dog for Advice

In this technique, use a visualization of a computer and monitor or a movie screen to contact an expert counselor who knows all the answers. You can choose any kind of person or being as your counselor though your Guide Dog is ideal. Plus feel free to invite in other experts and consultants for their input – even real people as well as dogs! So now, let's go. You can use the following as a general guide, or read it into a recorder and play it back as a guided fantasy.

To start the process, get relaxed. Then imagine that you have an office or other place in your house where you can go to find out whatever you want to know. It may be in the attic, basement, garage; any place you can be alone.

Wherever it is, take a walk there with your Guide Dog. Imagine him walking beside you, ready to help. As you walk there, notice what is around you. When you get to that room, open the door and go inside. As you look around, you see all kinds of books and papers. You see large stacks of computer printouts. Then, at the far wall, you notice a long desk and above it a computer console, with numerous gadgets and buttons. Above this you see a large monitor that looks like a movie screen. Just press a button, and you can see a movie of your own experiences on this screen.

Now, to work on resolving a problem or getting advice, press the button and you'll see the situation you want to resolve unfold on the screen. Or you may see the question you want to ask. Once the problem or question is clear, you can seek a solution or answer.

To obtain this answer, turn to your Guide Dog and ask for help. Tell him or her what is wrong and ask for advice on what to do or say to resolve matters.

Now listen as your Guide Dog tells you what to do. If the answer is simple, he or she will reply briefly. Or your counselor may ask you to press a button on your console, to see the solution. Then, some action you can take will appear on the screen.

If you have more questions, continue to ask them and your Guide Dog will reply. Again, wait for your answer in whatever form it comes. When you have no more questions, tell your Guide Dog you are done, and thank your Guide Dog for his or her help.

Then, turn off your computer console and leave your workshop. Return to the regular part of your house. As you do, return to normal consciousness and open your eyes.

Usually, you will have clear answers as a result of this process. However, if your Guide Dog didn't have any answers or asks you to wait, this means you don't have enough information or the situation is unclear. If so, wait a day or two and ask your questions again; or use another technique to obtain more information or increase your confidence, so you are in a better position to take action.

Taking a Journey to Find Your Answer

In this journey technique, you travel to the top of a mountain to learn your answers with the help of your Guide Dog and others you meet along the way. In some versions of this technique, the journey is to meet a wise man or woman who lives in the mountains. But, since this is the 21st century, not many wise men or women live in the mountains anymore. Besides, you've been learning to get help from your Guide Dog, so that's who'll help now. I've adapted this journey from one in *Mind Power*.

To take this journey, first get very relaxed and comfortable. Use this description as a general guide for your experience or record the journey and play it back while you listen.

This journey begins in the midst of a beautiful meadow. See yourself there surrounded by lush green foliage. Your Guide Dog is beside you. The air is clear and warmed by the sun. Nearby, you hear the soft buzz of bees and the chatter of birds. Off in the distance, you see a large mountain and walk toward it with your Guide Dog. As you walk, notice the tiny flowers. Little mushrooms pop up in the shade of trees. You can feel the carpet of moss beneath your feet. Cows grazing on the hillside low softly.

As you walk toward the mountain, the trees begin to thin out and you pass patches of grassland. The wind feels stronger and cooler. Now you pass a small stream. Sit down for a moment with your Guide Dog to relax. Let your feet dangle in the stream. Feel the water move past them. It's so relaxing, and you feel very peaceful. You sit very still and listen.

Now go on. As you walk uphill, note that the trees give way to bushes. You come to a clearing and look down on the meadow and valley below. Notice how far away it seems.

Now as you climb higher and higher, notice how the air begins to cool. Yet the sun shines on you directly and warms you. As you climb further, experience a sense of clarity and self-understanding, as you get farther and farther away from the things that usually concern you. It is as if you are leaving the world and all its cares behind. Realizing this, you feel an intense sense of peace.

Now you come near the top of the mountain, where you see a tall rock and tree. Go there with your Guide Dog and sit down by the tree. This rock and tree are the source of great wisdom.

Now, with your question clearly in mind, ask your Guide Dog, who will turn to the rock and tree, and listen for the answer. As your Guide Dog hears the answer, he will tell you, or you will hear the answer at the same time. Just listen to the answer.

If you have additional questions, go ahead and ask them. Again, your Guide Dog will turn to the rock and tree to obtain the answers.

Afterward, thank your Guide Dog for his help, and go back down the mountain as you came, and return to the meadow where you began your journey.

Asking Your Body – and Your Guide Dog – For Answers

Another way to get yes, no, and maybe answers is by asking your body, since your body holds the key to your subconscious, when you learn to read your body's cues and train your body to give them. A little nudge by your Guide Dog will help your body respond with those cues.

As with the technique of seeing the answer on your mental screen or hearing it from your inner voice, you need to do some initial practice to train your responses until they become automatic. In this case, you must physically move your body to get answers. But after some practice, you can visualize these bodily movements in your mind or can develop a voice inside you to answer for your body. Alternatively, you can learn to feel very subtle motions within your body, such as the speed of your pulse or your heartbeat.

One way to start asking your body for information is to train it to act like a pendulum, which will move forward and back to give you "yes" answers; to the side to give you "nos", and in a circle to give you "maybes" or "not sures." Your Guide Dog is there to give you that little nudge to get your body moving. To condition your body to respond this way, use the following technique.

> *Stand straight and imagine your body as a pendulum. See your Guide Dog standing close beside you.*
>
> *As your Guide Dog gives you a gentle push, sway backward and forward. That means 'yes". As your Guide Dog gives you another push, sway to the right and left. That means "no". Now with another push from your Guide Dog, sway in a circular motion.*
>
> *Go through this process several times, alternating the order in which you go forward and back, left and right, and move in a circular motion, so the signals become automatic.*
>
> *Then ask yourself some yes-no questions to which you know the answers. Your body, with a push from your Guide Dog, should respond with the appropriate swaying motion. Once it does this consistently, you are ready to begin asking it for answers.*
>
> *Ask your questions as yes-no questions, such as: "Is it in my best interest to do this?" or "Should I do this?" After you ask, observe how your Guide Dog pushes you and your body responds — with a back and forward yes motion, a side to side no, or a circular maybe. With*

practice, you should get clear yeses and nos. Once you do, you can decide whether to act accordingly.

If you get a lot of circular motions for maybes or get alternating yeses and no's to the same question, you may not be asking the question clearly or your conscious self may be getting in the way. To find out, ask: "'Is my question unclear?" or "Is my conscious self getting in the way?" If so, clarify or reframe your question, or push your conscious thoughts and feelings aside to let your inner self speak. Or ask your question another time.

At first, you will have to physically assume this pendulum position when you ask a question. But once you are familiar with this technique and consistently get clear answers, you can make it a mental process. Just imagine your body as a pendulum with your Guide Dog beside you and ask your question. Then observe how your body responds in your mind's eye, or listen to what your inner voice tells you about your body.

Later, you won't need to imagine the pendulum. You can merely ask your question and feel your body respond with a yes or a no or maybe.

New Ways to Just Have Fun

Besides these practical applications, you can use the Dog Type system to just have fun. How? Simply call on any of your dogs to join you when you participate in real life fun activities, especially when you're on your own, such as hiking the mountains, walking along a beach, or taking a swim. Or use a visualization to go on a mental journey or participate in a fun activity with one of your dogs. Imagine your dog is beside you as you experience this journey or activity.

Here are a few examples to get you started. Then, come up with other ways to have fun with your dogs.

- As you listen to music, imagine that your Top Dog or Guide Dog is with you. As he or she moves to the music, you feel the music even more intensely and vividly yourself.
- When you go to an art gallery, imagine that your Top Dog or Guide Dog is with you, commenting on the art you see as you move from piece to piece.
- When you participate in any activity by yourself – from going on a hike, swimming, or going for a run, imagine that your Top Dog or Guide is with you. Then, let your imagination go. For instance, as you run faster, imagine you are racing with your dog. As you find sea creatures along the beach, imagine that your dog is commenting on them.
- When you exercise, imagine that your Top Dog or Power Dog is beside you, cheering you on and giving you even more energy.
- Go on a mental journey with your dog. For example, imagine you are blasting off to outer space, and your Top Dog or Guide Dog is beside you. Or journey back in time to another place and age, and your Guide Dog is there to advise you and your Power Dog is there to protect you. Or think of other places you would like to visit, say on vacation.

In short, the possibilities for having fun with your dogs are endless. Just let your imagination go.

Still Other Ways to Work with the Dog Type System

Now that you've learned many methods for working with the Dog Type system, you can think of many other ways to use it. For example, call on your dogs to help you eliminate bad habits, improve your memory, increase your ability to concentrate and pay attention, help with your health, and more.

Plus you can find many ways to share and participate in these techniques with others. You can also use these techniques to help and counsel others, say by using the insights from your Guide Dogs and Top Dog to provide guidance. Or call on your Power Dog to assist you in helping to energize and motivate others.

   So what kind of dog are you? What kind of dogs are the people you interact with? And how can your dogs help you and others? Just call on your dogs and you're off and running. And if anyone tells you that "the world is going to the dogs", well, maybe that's a good thing to happen now, as you think about and work with your dogs in this new way.

CHAPTER 3: SUMMING UP AND EVEN MORE POSSIBILITIES

In the previous chapters, I have illustrated the many ways this system can be applied, from understanding yourself to improving your relationships with others. It can be used in one's personal life or in the workplace for a variety of everyday activities and just to have fun.

In short, this is a new system that can take its place alongside other systems for personal and organizational development – from Myers-Briggs to astrology and Tarot cards. A reason this approach of working with different dogs is so helpful is because for many thousands of years, dogs have been humans' closet companion, and they have been bred in hundreds of cultures for many different purposes – from being a tough hard-working dog to a loyal, affectionate companion.

Here I just want to sum up the major ways you can continue to work with this system to gain insights about yourself and your relationships. I'll conclude with a few suggestions on how to use this system in other ways – including just for fun.

For Self-Understanding and Personal Development

Since the dog you picked as your favorite (your Top Dog) or your next favorite dog (your Watch Dog) reflects the qualities you already have or would like to develop, some exercises to become more aware of these qualities can help you acquire or develop them. While you can do these exercises on your own, sharing with others can contribute to even broader insights, so if you can, set up a group to share your experiences. The major exercises to practice for greater self-understanding and personal development include these:

- Once you select your Top Dog and Watch Dog, take some time to think of the qualities associated with these dogs and how the choice reflects who you are. Pick any quality you want to work on experiencing and developing. You can do this as a "Top of Mind" exercise, coming up with the first idea you think of by looking through the dog profiles to see which one seems most right for you, or as a relaxed visualization where you see yourself expressing those qualities in various situations. This processing helps you think about the many qualities you have.
- Next think about the qualities you would like to further develop and pick one. Then, quickly think of or visualize a situation in which you would like to use that quality at home or in work, having more strength to do something or being a more outgoing, warm person. See yourself as already having that quality, and feel confident that you can express that quality effectively. Then, watch the scene play out before you. Notice what happens when you express that quality. After the visualization, notice how you felt about expressing that quality and ask yourself these questions: "How did that quality help me gain what I want? What can I do now to further develop that quality in my life?
- Now that you have identified the qualities to develop, put them into practice in everyday life in one of two ways:
  1. Visualize yourself with these qualities before you go into a situation and seek to express those qualities (i.e.: be warmer and more outgoing like a Cocker Spaniel; have more strength and endurance like a Bullmastiff);
  2. Set up a situation where you can express those qualities, possibly with people you don't already know (i.e.: join a group of strangers waiting somewhere, like in a bus terminal, so you can experiment with being warmer and more outgoing).
    - Call on your inner Guide Dog(s) for additional advice and/or ask your Power Dog(s) for more support,

particularly when seeking new ways to increase or use your power.

For Understanding and Improving Relationships

Since the type of dog you associate with others gives you insight into what they are like and how to better interact with them, some exercises to become more aware of these qualities and how to deal with others can help you do this. Plus you can gain additional help from your Guide Dogs, Power Dogs, and Rescue Dogs by doing these exercises on your own or sharing with others in a group. The major exercises to practice for greater understanding about others and how to have better relationships with them include:

- Imagine that someone you know at work or in your personal life is a dog and consider what dog would that person is. Then, consider what traits that dog would have.
- Think how you might better interact with this person in the future, based on the qualities you associate with this dog.
- Think about the types of dogs you most like to interact with and how this knowledge might guide you in the future, such as in deciding whether to initiate or remain in a close relationship with someone.
- Think about the how knowing a person's preferences for different dogs might help you put groups of people or teams together.
- Call on your Guide Dog(s) for additional advice and/or on your Power Dog(s) for their support, particularly when you are dealing with an already strong, powerful, and unfair person, such as a "Machiavellian" boss, who is interested in showing off what he or she has accomplished and taking all the credit for it.

For a Variety of Everyday Purposes

When it comes to everyday activities, you can use the system for just about anything, since you are calling on your Guide Dogs for advice; your Power dogs for power; and your Rescue Dogs for more assistance. In short, you are calling on whatever dog you associate with the qualities you feel will help in that situation – and if you are drawn to mixed breeds, well the more the merrier. Among the many activities where you can gain help, as previously described, you can call in the dogs to help you:
- Relax and calm down
- Increase your energy and power
- Increase your feelings of confidence and self-esteem
- Set and achieve goals
- Improve your skills
- Increase your creativity
- Resolve problems and make better decisions

In short, whenever you might use any other self-help system, you can apply this system – with a little extra help from your dogs.

Mostly Just for Fun

Finally, besides using these techniques for insight, personal development, and relationships building, you can use various techniques just for fun. You might gain some insight in the process, but otherwise, just enjoy. Some ways to have fun with these techniques include the following – and certainly, you can think of many more ideas. To get you started:
- After choosing your Top Dog and imagining what dog someone else is, imagine you are both interacting as dogs, and notice what happens. Are you playful? Warm? In a power struggle? Imagine the scene.

- Once you pick a dog for a person, imagine that you could change the person into another type of dog. As you interact with that person, notice what happens. For example, you go to talk to your usually tough Bulldog boss, but now he's gentle and playful like an Old English Sheepdog.

Still Other Ways to Use this System for Getting to Know Others and Having Fun

Here are a few last suggestions for having fun with this system and meeting and getting to know others.
- Put together a workshop based on any of these chapters, such as the two illustrated in this book. If the group is large enough, divide people into smaller groups based on the dog they pick as their Top Dog and the number of people in the group. Ideally, end up with groups with 4-6 people, and combine similar types of dogs together (for instance, combine everyone who has selected large, tough dogs into one group; people who have picked small, toy dogs into another. Then, focus the program around what people are interested in; choose appropriate exercises; adapt the techniques to suit the group, such as using visualization if people like this, or using "top of mind" responses if preferred.
- After each technique, invite people to share in their small group and with the group as a whole. You'll find that people enjoy sharing with others with similar choices as well as seeing how those in different groups do it differently. Creating teams is a great approach for a social mixer, too.
- Use the system to put on a fun singles event, where people choose their favorite or Top Dog. Then they move around meeting others who have made similar choices and at times mix and meet with people making a different choice. For

instance, imagine the German Shepherds meeting in one group, the Dobermans in another, the Poodles in a third. If a guy who's a German Shepherd wants to meet a woman who's a Poodle, there will be some time for cross-choice mingling, too.

- Use the system to create interactive social games. For instance, imagine a game where people pair up, spend a brief time talking, then each person puts the name of a dog he or she thinks the other person is on his or her back. Then, the game is for each person to figure out what dog he or she is by moving around from person to person and asking a single "yes" or "no" question of each one. The winner is the first person to discover and announce what kind of dog he or she is.
- Create an ad to meet others for friendship or dating based on the type of dog you each are. For example, a singles ad might go something like this: "I'm a German Shepherd looking for a Poodle."
- Have a "Come as Your Favorite Dog" party, in which everyone comes as their Top Dog. Plan a variety of fun games and skits where people participate as Top Dog. Or as an alternative make it a "Come as Your Underdog" party, and see what happens when everyone turns up as their least favorite dog.
- Use some exercises on understanding others for team-building or as a fun incentive to motivate the sales team.
- Put on a Dog Type program for people with dogs, and invite them to come with their dogs.
- And now…well, you get the picture. Keep going and think of even more fun ways to play with the Dog Type system – and let us know when you do. We'd like to include the ideas in a future book. So keep the ideas coming and have fun. Woof!

ABOUT THE AUTHOR

GINI GRAHAM SCOTT, Ph.D., J.D., is a nationally known writer, consultant, speaker, and seminar leader, specializing in social trends, popular culture, business and work relationships, and professional and personal development. She has published over 50 books on diverse subjects with major publishers. She has worked with dozens of clients on memoirs, self-help, and popular business books, as well as film scripts. Her websites include www.changemakerspublishingandwriting.com and www.ginigrahamscott.com. She is a Huffington Post regular columnist, commenting on social trends, new technology, business, and everyday life at www.huffingtonpost.com/gini-graham-scott.

She is the founder of Changemakers Publishing featuring books on social trends, work, business, psychology, and self-help, which has published over 100 Print, e-books, and audiobooks. She has licensed several dozen books for foreign sales, including in the UK, Russia, Korea, Spain, Indonesia, and Japan.

She has written numerous books on creativity and visualization, including *Mind Power: Picture Your Way to Success; The Empowered Mind: How to Harness the Creative Force within You;* and *Want It, See It, Get It!*

She has received national media exposure for her books, including appearances on *Good Morning America, Oprah,* and *CNN.* She has been the producer and host of a talk show series, CHANGEMAKERS, featuring interviews on social trends.

Scott is active in a number of community and business groups, including the Lafayette, Danville, and Pleasant Hill Chambers of Commerce. She is a graduate of the prestigious Leadership in Contra Costa County program and is a member of a BNI group in Walnut Creek, B2B groups in Danville and Walnut Creek, and many other business networking groups. She is the organizer of six Meetup groups in the film and publishing industries with over 6000 members in Los Angeles and the San Francisco Bay Area. She also does workshops and seminars on the topics of her books.

She received her Ph.D. from the University of California, Berkeley, and her J.D. from the University of San Francisco Law School. She has received five MAs at Cal State, East Bay, including most recently an MA in Communications. She will be starting an additional MA program in history there in the fall of 2017.

CHANGEMAKERS PUBLISHING
3527 Mt. Diablo Blvd., #273
Lafayette, CA 94549
changemakers@pacbell.net . (925) 385-0608
www.changemakerspublishingandwriting.com

www.ingramcontent.com/pod-product-compliance
Lightning Source LLC
Chambersburg PA
CBHW071543080526
44588CB00011B/1769